Writers & their Work

Sir Walter Ralegh

by Agnes M. C. Latham

No. 177

Soldier, seaman, explorer, courtier and poet, Sir Walter Ralegh was one of the greatest, most gifted and most enigmatic figures of his age. He won and lost its highest prize, the favour of Queen Elizabeth. He led abortive expeditions to discover the legendary gold of the Incas with which to buy it back, yet noted with appreciation in the midst of failure the customs of the Indians, the geography of the land. Rejected by James I, he was soon brought down by his enemies. Miss Latham, in this perceptive study, underlines the contradictions in Ralegh's character and actions, nowhere more manifest than in his writing in which he combined 'truth with fiction, a sombre pessimism with a contagious zest for life'. In his beliefs 'he belittled man, undermined worldly values, yet set all within the structure of God's providence'. And in the 'passionate disarray' of his verse can be detected notes of violence, of concentrated scorn, and of deep melancholy.

Agnes Latham is Reader in English at Bedford College in the University of London. She has edited Ralegh's poems, and her special field is the late sixteenth and early seventeenth century.

20p net

SIR WALTER RALEGH
*from a painting by an unknown artist
National Portrait Gallery*

SIR WALTER RALEGH

by

AGNES M. C. LATHAM

PUBLISHED FOR
THE BRITISH COUNCIL
BY LONGMAN GROUP LTD

248698

LONGMAN GROUP LTD
Longman House, Burnt Mill, Harlow, Essex

*Associated companies, branches and
representatives throughout the world*

First published 1964
Reprinted with minor amendments and additions to Bibliography 1971
© Agnes M. C. Latham, 1964, 1971

*Printed in Great Britain by
F. Mildner & Sons, London, EC1*

SBN 0 582 01177 9

CONTENTS

I. INTRODUCTION	5
II. POET	8
III. SEAMAN	15
IV. EMPIRE BUILDER	18
V. HISTORIAN	24
VI. 'ATHEIST'	29
A SELECT BIBLIOGRAPHY	37

¶Sir Walter Ralegh was born at Hayes Barton, Devonshire, in 1554. He was condemned to death and executed at Westminster on 29 October, 1618.

SIR WALTER RALEGH

I. INTRODUCTION

S IR WALTER RALEGH is valued above all as a man of action. His intellectual and literary gifts were an added ornament, proper to the renaissance concept of a fully developed personality. Conversely, his many and varied occupations as soldier, seaman, courtier and explorer, seem to have increased his stature as a man of letters. His writings were almost always a by-product of his active life, designed to recommend his projects, to call attention to their success or to excuse their failure. He wrote because he had something he very urgently wanted to say, and this intimate personal urgency is one of the dominant characteristics of his work. It is reflected in the poignant, melancholy rhythms of *The History of the World* and the passionate disarray of his verse, and equally in the direct, near-colloquial narrative of *The Last Fight of the Revenge* and *The Discovery of Guiana*. He never uses fine writing for its own sake but rises to meet what seems to him a great occasion. Because he was living a full life in an expanding world he often met with great occasions. Adverse critics contend that he manufactured them—that he used his literary gifts to heighten any difficulties he encountered and to distort the truth in his own interest. Nobody denies him imagination, but it is perhaps true that he lacked judgement.

Walter Ralegh was born in 1554, a younger son of a Devonshire gentleman, with his own way to make in the world, backed by a host of West Country kinsfolk who were doing the same thing. As a young man he fought on the Protestant side in the French Wars of Religion and in the Desmond Rebellion in Ireland. When he was not fighting he spent some time in residence at Oriel College, Oxford, and at the Inns of Court, in London. All the time his eyes were fixed upon Court favour, the highest prize which any fortune hunter could possibly hope to win, and by 1580 he had made it his. He became first favourite of the Queen. That same vitality and vigour, charm and intelligence, that personal urgency which still survives in his written work, must have had twice the force when embodied in the man himself. Elizabeth could not resist it.

He flourished in her grace, but it was a full-time occupation, and personal adventure was for the moment in abeyance. In 1592 his fortunes took a spectacular turn for the worse, on the discovery that he had secretly married one of the Queen's maids-of-honour, a treachery his royal mistress could not forgive. The young Earl of Essex, who had been disputing with him for the Queen's affection, was there to fill his place. Ralegh was left to strive for distinction in the war at sea, taking part in maritime expeditions against Spain and leading a voyage of exploration to South America, where he hoped to found an English colony in Guiana to be the nucleus of an overseas empire. As reigning favourite, arrogant and acquisitive (he had very expensive tastes, founding colonies being one of them) he had been far from popular. After his fall from favour he could be openly abused and derided. He was suspected of engineering the downfall of Essex, but that rash young nobleman suffered more from the encouragement of his friends than from the machinations of Sir Walter Ralegh.

When, in 1603, the old Queen died and King James VI of Scotland became King James I of England, Ralegh was marked down for destruction. His enemies wanted to finish with him and James did not want to start. The King was content to accept the popular estimate, enhanced by a deliberate whispering campaign in high circles. Before long Ralegh was charged with complicity in a plot to dethrone the King, make peace with Spain and exact tolerance for Roman Catholics. The nature and extent of his complicity in these ill-organized projects has never been made clear. They do not seem such as would appeal to him, but there was sufficient evidence, largely supplied by his friend, Lord

Cobham, to convict him. King James accorded him a last-minute reprieve and confined him for thirteen years in the Tower, while he made peace overtures to Spain in his own good time.

The new policy of appeasement was not too well liked. There were those who thought that Elizabeth's long struggle with King Philip should end in a knock-out blow rather than in a negotiated peace. Subjected to increasing pressure, James in 1616 agreed to release though not to pardon his prisoner, who for some time had been offering to open a gold mine in Guiana without giving just cause of offence to Spain. The Spanish Ambassador intimated strongly that he was offended even before the expedition sailed. No compensating mine was found. The English destroyed a Spanish outpost which lay in their way, protesting that they had not known it was there, though there was every reason why they should have known and they probably did. Ralegh's young son was shot dead in the skirmish.

Ralegh himself was in no position to exercise authority, though he had to bear the blame for everything that happened. He had been near to dying of a tropical fever during the voyage and stayed at Trinidad, while his lieutenant, Lawrence Keymis, led the prospectors inland. On his return, Ralegh reproached him bitterly for not opening the mine, whereupon Keymis retired to his cabin and took his own life. Ralegh returned empty-handed to an England which was deeply curious about the venture and not wholly unsympathetic. His defence of his proceedings was eagerly read. His letters home, recounting the disasters of the voyage, were copied and passed from hand to hand, together with the verses he was said to have written on the fly-leaf of his Bible the night before he was beheaded. For James did not spare him, and his death took on the air of a martyrdom, or at any rate of a tragedy, in which he played his central part to admiration.

He appealed to the middle seventeenth century as a victim of Stuart tyranny. They saw him as anti-Spanish, anti-

Catholic, and even anti-royalist, a witness in *The Discovery of Guiana* to England's colonial future and in *The History of the World* to a divine providence guiding events. Thus, in a way which would have amazed contemporaries, accustomed to hearing him called 'damnable atheist' and 'mischievous Machiavel', he became a hero. A small sheaf of minor works circulated as *The Remains of Sir Walter Raleigh*. Modern research has inevitably modified the picture. Sir Julian Corbett has queried his naval expertise. S. R. Gardiner is convinced of his guilt in 1618, and has some damaging documents to show relating to the last Guiana voyage. Mario Praz finds his policy machiavellian, and he is credited with presiding over a club of freethinkers called the School of Night. The latter charges do nothing to dim the vivid colours in which he is usually presented. The many biographies which attempt to unravel the riddle of his personality testify to its enduring fascination.

II. POET

Ralegh's poetry has survived only in stray pieces, sifted from the anthologies and commonplace books of the time, with subscriptions of dubious value. He preserved his anonymity more jealously than most Elizabethans, anxious as they were to appear gentlemen, with minds above money. He had more reason. The lady he adored was the greatest lady in the land. Much poetry was addressed to the Queen in her public character. Ralegh addressed her personally and privately in the character of platonic mistress. This was not matter for the book-stalls. His poetic reputation was confined to a select circle. It included George Puttenham, who had some first-hand knowledge of his verses, since he quotes from them in his *Art of English Poetry* (1589), describing Ralegh's vein as 'most lofty, insolent and passionate'. Spenser was also among the privileged few. In 1589 Ralegh visited him in Ireland and listened to readings from unpublished verse, after which he read in exchange some of his own. It was, says Spenser,

> all a lamentable lay,
> Of great unkindness, and of usage hard,
> Of Cynthia the Ladie of the sea,
> Which from her presence faultless him debarr'd ...
> Right well he sure did plain:
> That could great Cynthia's sore displeasure break,
> And move to take him to her grace again.
> 'Colin Clouts Come Home Againe' (1595).

The character of Timias, who loves the maiden-huntress Belphoebe though he can never possess her, and is banished her sight when he turns momentarily aside, is Spenser's idealized picture, in the third book of *The Faerie Queene*, of Ralegh and Elizabeth. He gives the story a happy ending, with Timias forgiven, and it would appear that in 1589 Ralegh, who had retired to Ireland in temporary disfavour, did indeed soothe the Queen's vexation with some plaintive verses which have not survived outside Spenser's description of them. In 1592 there came a rift which verses could not heal. Elizabeth Throckmorton, one of the Queen's maids of honour, gave birth to a son. Ralegh was the father and Essex the godfather. Before long it was common knowledge that Cynthia's devoted servant was a married man. It is possible to sympathize with both sides. He was a man approaching forty who wanted a home and children, she a woman of sixty, burdened with the crown of England, who felt that she had been fooled with sweet words. Ralegh tried to heal the wound, as he had before, with more words. Among the Cecil Papers at Hatfield House there is a manuscript fragment of some five hundred lines in his hand entitled 'The Eleventh and Twelfth Books of the Ocean to Cynthia'. Presumably he hoped that his friend Sir Robert Cecil might find occasion to show them to the Queen and that he could perform again the feat of 1589. It was a far-fetched hope which failed. If the verses seem inordinately passionate, it is worth reflecting how very much Ralegh lost when he lost the Queen's regard.

The Hatfield fragments remain almost the only undoubted specimens of Ralegh's verse. The title suggests that they are a continuation of the 'lamentable lay' known to Spenser, though it is difficult to imagine how ten earlier books could have been filled with matter so abstract. There is no narrative thread. The lines display only a perpetual flux and reflux of contrary feeling, as the poet remembers happier days and then recalls the painful present, only to deny the reality of present pain and grief in the contemplation of an eternity of beauty to which he must needs respond with an undying affection. Sensual love and sensual beauty, which are ephemeral, are strongly contrasted with their opposites:

> And though strong reason hold before mine eyes
> The images and forms of worlds past
> Teaching the cause why all those flames that rise
> From forms external, can no longer last
>
> Than that those seeming beauties hold in prime,
> Love's ground, his essence, and his empery,
> All slaves to age, and vassals unto time,
> Of which repentance writes the tragedy;
>
> But this, my heart's desire could not conceive,
> Whose love outflew the fastest flying time;
> A beauty that can easily deceive
> Th'arrest of years, and creeping age outclimb,
>
> A spring of beauties which time ripeth not
> Time that but works on frail mortality,
> A sweetness which woe's wrongs outwipeth not,
> Whom love hath chose for his divinity,
>
> A vestal fire that burns but never wasteth,
> That loseth naught by giving light to all,
> That endless shines eachwhere, and endless lasteth,
> Blossoms of pride that can nor fade nor fall.

In spite of its vague and transcendental manner the poem plainly relates to the current situation. It tells of 'the tokens hung on breast and kindly worn', the showers of grace

> Which now to others do their sweetness send . . .
> Filling their barns with grain and towers with treasure,

and how, when the writer attempted

> To seek new worlds, for gold, for praise, for glory,
> To try desire, to try love severed far,
> When I was gone she sent her memory
> More strong than were ten thousand ships of war
>
> To call me back, to leave great honour's thought,
> To leave my friends, my fortune, my attempt
> To leave the purpose I so long had sought . . .

The last book 'Entreating of Sorrow' breaks off in the middle of a line and the fragment as a whole, though it is copied in a fair hand, is disorderly, reflecting what is perhaps an intentionally assumed desperation. The writer would like the reader to think that he is half crazy and that his lines are something overheard rather than formally stated. They have a cloudy magnificence and power but along with it a curious limpness. The poet seems to be inviting the emotion to take him where it will and attempts little control. C. S. Lewis speaks of 'the monotony, the insanity, and the rich, dark colours of an obsessive despair'. Metrically the verse is extremely fluent. There is a vaguely pastoral framework, perhaps continuing something in earlier books, much imagery of trees and fruit and corn and flowers, and some bold similes.

The lax construction and the absence of anything resembling climax are not characteristic of Ralegh's writing. His manner in lyrics tends to be terse, pointed and epigrammatic. An instance is 'Conceit begotten by the eyes', in which he treats his favourite theme of ephemeral passion':

> As ships in ports desired are drowned,
> As fruit once ripe, then falls to ground,
> As flies that seek for flames, are brought
> To cinders by the flames they sought:
> So fond Desire when it attains
> The life expires, the woe remains.

A poem which is notable for its abrupt, contemptuous rhythms is 'The Lie', in which he savagely reveals the corruptions of society and forces upon it again and again the ultimate insult of 'the lie'.

> Go soul, the body's guest,
>   Upon a thankless errand,
> Fear not to touch the best,
>   The truth shall be thy warrant;
> Go, since I needs must die
>   And give the world the lie.

The tradition that he was the author of this not very typical poem is possibly a tribute to his personality, his supposed disrespect for established sanctities. It is the kind of poem people could imagine him writing. A similar tradition assigns to him a much stranger poem, 'The passionate man's pilgrimage', in which the speaker is about to be beheaded and imagines his journey to a better land, where justice is not corrupt,

> For there Christ is the King's Atturney:
> Who pleads for all without degrees
> And he hath angels, but no fees.

If it is his, it must represent his feelings when in 1603 he awaited the headsman's axe and reflected upon the injustice and brutality of his trial. Where 'The Lie' shocks with its matter, this shocks by its manner, the irregular verse form, the odd juxtaposition of legal terms and eschatology, the way the writer abandons himself in a kind of trance to chance rhythms and word associations:

> And by the happy blissful way
> More peaceful pilgrims I shall see,
> That have shook off their gowns of clay,
> And go apparelled fresh like me.
> I'll bring them first
> To slake their thirst,
> And then to taste those nectar suckets
> At the clear wells
> Where sweetness dwells,
> Drawn up by saints in crystal buckets.

It is hard to judge poetry written under stress, which may not be characteristic of the author's normal manner. One of the interesting things about Ralegh's verse is the number of times he seems to be writing under the pressure of strong emotion, with a rather strange abandon. An instance, close in both matter and manner to the last books of *Cynthia*, is the little colloquy he devised upon the basis of the ballad of Walsingham:

> She hath left me here all alone,
>   All alone as unknown,
> Who sometimes did me lead with herself,
>   And me loved as her own.

The verses which he wrote in 1618, in expectation of death, are in another category, completely controlled. This time his sentence came as no surprise to him, and he met it with great gallantry. The verses were just one gesture among many. Sympathizers, who made endless copies of them, might not have been so much impressed had they realized that he was recalling a stanza of an earlier poem, to which he has added a staid and devout couplet:

> Even such is time which takes in trust
> Our youth, our joys, and all we have,
> And pays us but with age and dust:
> Who in the dark and silent grave
> When we have wandered all our ways
> Shuts up the story of our days.
> And from which earth and grave and dust
> The Lord shall raise me up I trust.

The earlier piece lamented the passing of youth and beauty and sensuous delight and offered no comfort for it. It is a not uncommon mood with Ralegh, and is displayed perfectly in his answer to Marlowe's 'Passionate Shepherd':

> Time drives the flocks from field to fold,
> When rivers rage, and rocks grow cold,
> And Philomel becometh dumb,
> The rest complain of cares to come.
>
> The flowers do fade, and wanton fields
> To wayward winter reckoning yields,
> A honey tongue, a heart of gall,
> Is fancy's spring, but sorrow's fall.

Too little of his poetry has survived for it to be easy to make any general assessment of it, to trace influences or suggest sources. It changes before the reader's eyes from the stilted angry couplets prefaced to Gascoigne's satire, *The Steel Glass*, in 1576, through the smoothness of 'Nature that washt her hands in milk' and the terseness of 'Conceit begotten by the eyes', to the turbulence of 'The Books of the Ocean's Love to Cynthia' and the startling free associations of 'The passionate man's pilgrimage', to the grave serenity of 'Even such is Time'. The one quality these pieces have in common is their disillusion. Contemporaries stress their sweetness. To Spenser Ralegh's verse was 'honied' and 'with nectar sprinkled'. It has in addition qualities of violence and of concentrated scorn, and a note of deep melancholy. Tucker Brooke has described it as 'the froth that rises where unplumbed waters break on adamant'.

III. SEAMAN

The problem of establishing a reliable canon affects Ralegh's prose as well as his poetry. It has too long been taken for granted that all the pieces collected and published under his name in the mid-seventeenth century (one of them, *The Cabinet Council*, by John Milton) were his. These doubts, however, do not arise in regard to his three best known works, *The Last Fight of the Revenge*, *The Discovery of Guiana*, and *The History of the World*.

The first two are propaganda pieces. Ralegh was early convinced that England, threatened by the might of Catholic Spain, should not defend herself by sending reluctant recruits to fight land battles in France, Ireland and the Low Countries, but should open a naval offensive concentrated upon cutting Spanish trade routes to the New World. It was not to be expected that the Queen and her more conservative ministers would have much grasp of advanced naval strategy. Even today historians contend that England's first line of defence was the continental coast, and that it would have been most ill-advised to exchange the European land-theatre for the experimental hazards of the Atlantic. Nonetheless Elizabeth was not averse to a supplementary policy of naval pressure, the more so because the seamen could pay themselves out of the profits of their privateering. Her Majesty, Ralegh complained long after, 'did all by halves'.

In 1591, Lord Thomas Howard was awaiting the homecoming of the Spanish treasure fleet, which had been forced for fear of English commerce-raiders to winter at Havana. He was watering and cleaning his ships at the Azores, when he was surprised by an armada from Spain, which was King Philip's very expectable retort to English depredations among his merchantmen. The largest ship in Howard's squadron, the *Revenge*, was commanded by Ralegh's Cornish cousin, Sir Richard Grenville. Grenville was the last to get away, and finding himself cut off from his commander by the Spanish fleet, elected to sail through the middle of it with all his guns blazing rather than to turn and run before the wind. To run would have been an entirely proper naval manœuvre in no way parallel to 'running' in a land battle. Grenville, always something of a fire-eater, preferred the other course and after a prolonged battle against spectacular odds lost the Queen's best ship to the enemy.

Ralegh's pamphlet, published anonymously, followed so promptly upon the action that he was still ignorant of the fact that Grenville had died of wounds and been buried at sea, after which a cyclone of exceptional violence had battered the Spanish ships, thus indicating that either God or the devil was on Grenville's side. The pamphlet was called *A Report of the Truth of the Fight about the Iles of Açores this last Summer betwixt the Revenge, one of Her Majesties Shippes, and an Armada of the King of Spaine*, but is generally known by its running head as *The Last Fight of the Revenge at Sea*. Hakluyt reprinted it with his *Voyages* in 1598 and acknowledged Ralegh as the author. It would be natural to think that he was writing specifically in defence of his cousin but the text does not bear this out. Though Grenville, with great skill and plausibility, is transformed from a hothead into a hero, Ralegh's main concern is with the honour of England, the morale of her seamen, and the importance of the war at sea. Whoever had commanded the *Revenge* (for a time he was hoping to command her himself) he would have made the same case with the same urgency. He is not expert yet in the handling of prose. His sentences are often top-heavy and repetitive, but he is already a master of the telling phrase and gives a very strong sense of first hand participation in the events he is describing. Through the incidents he selects and the emphasis he lays on them, he contrives to impose an epic pattern upon what might in hostile hands have been a sorry tale of the loss of a capital ship, elevating it, as Bacon puts it, 'even to the height of an heroical fable'. A plainness and directness in the writing, together with a convincing show of impartiality and fair-mindedness (except towards the enemy, who could not expect it) give the narrative great power. All that can be objected against Grenville is in fact stated, but the reader responds in spite of it to the gallantry of the unequal encounter. Grenville need not have exposed his ship:

> The other course had been the better, and might right well have answered in so great an impossibility of prevailing. Notwithstanding, out of the greatness of his mind, he could not be persuaded.

Thereafter the battle is described in a narrative calculated to make a 'pure navy' man wince. Grenville had wilfully exchanged the new strategy of long range gunnery and manœuvrable ships for a hand-to-hand encounter through the night. This was exactly the kind of fighting which the Spaniards expected and for which they were equipped. Nonetheless, he held them off for an astonishingly long time, and Ralegh's rhetoric is equal to his theme. In its way and before its time, it is a piece of brilliant journalism:

> But as the day increased, so our men decreased: and as the light grew more, by so much more grew our discomforts. For none appeared in sight but enemies, saving one small ship called the *Pilgrim*, commanded by Jacob Whiddon, who hovered all night to see the success; but in the morning bearing with the *Revenge*, was hunted like a hare among many ravenous hounds, but escaped. All the powder of the *Revenge* to the last barrel was now spent, all her pikes broken, forty of her best men slain, and the most part of the rest hurt. In the beginning of the fight she had but one hundred free from sickness, and four score and ten sick, laid in hold upon the ballast. A small troop to man such a ship, and a weak garrison to resist so mighty an army. By those hundred all was sustained, the volleys, boardings and enterings of fifteen ships of war besides those which beat her at large.

The statement that the ammunition was exhausted does not tally with the last phase of the story, in which the survivors successfully bargained for their lives in exchange for the ship, after locking the master gunner in his own gun-room lest he should obey Sir Richard's orders to split and sink her. Since he seemed only too ready to do so, he clearly had some powder at his disposal. Ralegh has no fault to find with the men, who had fought a good fight. Rehearsing their commonsense arguments, he tranquilly observes that these won the day, 'it being no hard matter to dissuade men from death to life'. This double vision is characteristic of him. He could see the practical necessities that coexist with heroic potentialities. His idealism is the stronger for being based in fact and shot with a faint astringent cynicism. He used his imagination as an instrument for discerning truth as well as for heightening and manipulating it. It is because of this paradoxical clearsightedness that he could make poetry out of disillusion.

A lively and very partisan account of the expedition against Cadiz, in which Ralegh served under Essex in 1596, exists in manuscript and was printed in 1700. Various manuscript fragments relate to the navy and naval affairs. Ralegh projected a full-scale naval history for Prince Henry, but it is doubtful if he advanced far with it.

IV. EMPIRE BUILDER

The Discovery of Guiana illustrates very plainly Ralegh's double mastery of fact and fiction. It gave him a bad name among contemporaries, as well as enchanting the world, then and ever since. It is a very much more substantial work than the pamphlet on the *Revenge*. It was published in 1596, with his name on the title page, and is based upon his own experience. It might appear at first sight to be purely personal propaganda, but the plan Ralegh recommends was well beyond the resources of any private individual. Quite simply, he proposed that England should take over South America, beginning with the only region not effectively colonized by Spain: the country watered by the Orinoco and its tributaries, then known as Guiana. The terrain which Ralegh actually traversed, from the mouth of the Orinoco to the Caroni river, is now part of Venezuela. It was a further step in the Spanish war, and required the support of Queen and country. No such support was forthcoming and we should perhaps be thankful, for it would have been a tremendous undertaking, and there is no doubt that here as elsewhere Ralegh's optimism leapt ahead of rational expectation. He was not ignorant of colonizing, having twice dispatched settlers to Virginia. Their fate—the first came home and the second mysteriously disappeared in the wilderness—might have given him pause. Yet on his behalf it must be admitted that the Virginian venture was ultimately successful, though not before it had passed into the hands of a merchant syndicate.

When Ralegh colonized Virginia he was settling newfound land. His policy in Guiana was more aggressive. He had come to realize that casual commerce-raiding would never effectively stop the flow of gold and silver to Spain. What England needed was what Spain had in abundance, land bases from which to operate. He had reason to think that behind the dense forests of the Orinoco lay a secret empire of the Incas. Its capital city, Manoa, situated on a vast inland sea, was known to the Spaniards as El Dorado. He had carefully studied Spanish chronicles, read Spanish letters seized at sea, and sifted the gossip of West Country ports. The exploits of Cortez and Pizarro provided encouraging parallels. And yet the whole idea was a myth, which with a few days to spare Ralegh himself could have exploded. The great lake had no existence apart from seasonal floods in the high valleys. Objects of wrought gold produced by obliging Indians were relics of the Chibcha civilization of Colombia, out of which the Spaniards had already carved the Kingdom of New Granada. There was no truth in the story that some of the Inca princes had escaped and founded a new empire as rich as the old.

Ralegh's strategic plan was bold and brilliant. He intended to invade the Inca empire with the help of the borderers, who claimed to have been dispossessed. Then, having established a benevolent rule, the English could lead all Guiana against the Spanish colonies to the west of it, mobilizing the deep resentment of the natives against the brutal *conquistadores*. This meant that Ralegh's own conduct, in contrast, had to be kindly and protective. He sang Elizabeth's praises—and who could do it better than he? She was stronger than the hated *Castellani* and had freed many nations from their tyranny. 'The like and a more large discourse I made to the rest of the nations both in my passing to Guiana, and to those of the borders, so as in that part of the world', he reports delightedly, 'her majesty is very famous, whom they now call *Ezrabeta Cassipuna Aquerewana*, which is as much as Elizabeth, the great princess, or greatest commander.'

One of the pleasantest aspects of the *Discovery* is Ralegh's sympathy with the native Indians and his crusading fervour on their behalf. Their inferiority is in no way stressed, for they were to be enlisted as allies. In 1618, his argument that Guiana was English was based largely upon their power to enter into contracts and dispose of their own land by treaty with Europeans. He was genuinely charmed by their simple dignity. 'The tawny women', he noted, were 'excellently favoured, which came among us without deceit, stark naked.' Old chief Topiawari was touching in his grief for an only son lost in battle and he proved unexpectedly shrewd in council. His picturesque phraseology was worth reproducing:

He remembered in his father's time when he was very old, and himself a young man, that there came down into that large valley of Guiana a nation from so far off as the Sun slept (for such were his own words), with so great a multitude as they could not be numbered nor resisted, and that they wore large coats and hats of crimson colour, which colour he expressed by showing a piece of red wood wherewith my tent was supported, and that they were . . . . those that had slain and rooted out so many of the ancient people as there are leaves in the wood upon all the trees.

Significantly, Ralegh never reproaches the Indians with their barbarous religion nor congratulates himself upon the prospect of saving souls. He takes an intelligent interest in their customs and recounts them with tolerant understanding. It surprised him to find that they warred for women and not for gold, but he thought it over and saw that it made sense in a sparsely populated country.

The native *caçiques*, on their side, were captivated by his persuasive tongue. He could address them in their own heroic terms, and not without that necessary component of primitive heroism, much practical good sense. All the time, he carefully concealed the gold lust which was going to attract colonists, and freely distributed English coins as tokens from the Queen. An attempt to recoup by sacking the Spanish settlement at Cumaná was beaten off with heavy losses. This was an uncomfortable incident which Ralegh touches on lightly. The expedition, in consequence, came home little the richer and was early discredited. Ralegh may have convinced himself too easily that he could preserve good relations with the natives once Guiana was thrown open to English settlers, but it is plain, nonetheless, that he was thinking in terms larger than petty gain.

Part of *The Discovery of Guiana* is narrative, part descriptive (in terms which range from the geographical to the lyrical), part is a defence against charges of deliberate deceit and gross gullibility, and part is an eloquent statement of policy. By 'discovery' Ralegh means the opening and exploring of the country. He was not claiming to be the first to enter it. On the contrary, he rehearses the history of early Spanish expeditions with a strong sense of the drama inherent in them. He owed a good deal to current literature of the New World with which he was very familiar. His personal narrative presumably originated in some kind of journal of the voyage.

Though it has often been challenged, the book is basically accurate. If there is deceit, the writer had first deceived himself. Ralegh believed in the 'mighty, rich and beautiful empire of Guiana', and it is very hard for the reader not to share his delusion, as he confidently retails the information he had gathered from the border tribes, and from Antonio de Berrio, Governor of Trinidad, who spent a lifetime seeking El Dorado and died still believing in it. Ralegh admits that his own party never entered the secret empire and he does not claim to have spoken face to face with anyone who had been in Manoa. He dallies pleasurably with stories of Amazons, remote sisters of *Ezrabeta Cassipuna Aquerewana*, which may well have had some foundation in tribal custom as well as in classical history. He gives details of the Ewaipanoma, 'the men whose heads do grow beneath their shoulders', much in the spirit that modern explorers report on the Abominable Snowman. He was struck by the unanimity with which the Indians asserted their existence, and the odd way in which it corroborated Sir John Mandeville. But he goes no further than giving the reader his own reasons for crediting these wonders. He does not pose as an eyewitness.

His suppressions are in fact more dangerous than his assertions. E. G. M. Taylor accuses him of concealing 'the twofold climatic pulse—the change of season marked by the onset of the rains, and by the dangerous swelling of the waters, yet not by any cooling of the air'. The health of his party seems nonetheless to have been excellent. They were a close knit and efficient company, nearly all from the West Country. Ralegh praises the food available—fish, game, fruit, maize, cassava bread and native wines. He finds hammocks comfortable and convenient. His interest in new drugs is excited by native balsams and by the lethal arrow-poison, curare. Any hint that the rocks are metalliferous is exploited for rather more than it is worth, but he knows how gold occurs, in hard white spar or else in alluvial deposits.

The book went through many editions and was translated into Latin, Dutch and French. It was read as an up-to-the-minute news item, as a story of adventure, as a description of a strange country and as a practical prospectus for fortune hunters. But over and above all these it has an enduring charm, supplied by the same hand which shaped *The Last*

Fight of the Revenge into a heroic paradigm. This time it was not epic but a kind of exotic pastoral. The land, the beauty of the land and the promise of the land are what stay in the reader's mind, the brightness and newness of the brave New World. Every corner turned is in itself a small discovery:

> I never saw a more beautiful country nor more lively prospects, hills so raised here and there over the valleys, the river winding into divers branches, the plains adjoining without bush or stubble, all fair green grass, the ground of hard sand easy to march on either for horses or foot, the deer crossing every path, the birds toward the evening singing on every tree with a thousand several tunes, cranes and herons of white, crimson, and carnation perching on the river's side, the air fresh with a gentle easterly wind, and every stone that we stooped to take up promised gold or silver by his complexion.

The unspoiled country, the courtesy of its inhabitants, the golden city always just behind the next mountain range entered into the English imagination, to be reflected in Prospero's enchanted island and in Milton's Eden.

In 1617 Ralegh set sail once more, in a magnificently equipped vessel called the *Destiny*, which had cost him rather more than he had, and with a number of none too reliable consorts, the nature of the voyage and of its leader being not such as to attract sober spirits. It would appear from the available evidence that he was not going to be too particular how he got gold provided he got it. There was talk of his being joined by Flemish ships, and he certainly planned to use Frenchmen. If these took to privateering or burned a Spanish outpost, they could account for it to governments less tied than that of England to policies of appeasement. The question of what mine or mines he aimed at, how soundly grounded his hopes were, and whether he had intended from the beginning to take to privateering if the mines failed, provided subjects for hot debate, as does his excuse for the destruction of the town of San Thomé, which barred the way to a mine previously said to be in unoccupied territory.

The documents relative to the last Guiana expedition have been printed in one volume by V. T. Harlow. They include the letters Ralegh wrote to his wife and sponsors, his famous *Apology for the Voyage to Guiana*, and the co-called *Little Apology*, which was a letter to his cousin Sir George Carew. All these circulated freely in manuscript at the time. The note of personal urgency and personal commitment is naturally at its strongest in them. *The Apology* was written in great haste, under cover of a simulated bout of sickness. The arguments, recast in 1889 and shorn of emotion, were used as part of the British answer to territorial claims by Venezuela and as such they failed to convince. Harlow prints from a large number of Spanish documents which were officially transcribed at this time and which reveal curious and unexpected aspects of the expedition. What the Venezuelan case amounts to in sum is that exploration and colonization are two different things. The English never settled in the country. In 1618 it was not too late to claim that they were in process of settling and that they had the good will of the native *caçiques*, whereas the Spaniards had effected no more than a precarious military occupation. The country has in fact yielded gold in fair quantity and some diamonds. At present it is exploiting rich deposits of iron. The flooding of the rivers, which so hampered Ralegh's party, has proved a serious hindrance to progress.

V. HISTORIAN

The History of the World was composed during Ralegh's thirteen years' imprisonment in the Tower. He was allowed to have his books and to employ secretaries and amanuenses. Inevitably there was some envious gossip, to which Ben Jonson contributed, suggesting that he had done little of the work himself or had not made his indebtedness sufficiently plain. Contemporaries, anxious only to have their own contributions recognized, did not criticize his reliance upon compendiums already published, which was considerable in places, and indeed is hardly surprising. He had no Hebrew and not much Greek, reading Greek authors as much as possible in Latin translations. His French was fluent. He read and presumably spoke Spanish and he cannot have been without Italian. He had time on his hands and we know from his friend Sir Robert Cecil that he could 'toil terribly'.

His plan was comprehensive, beginning with the Creation. He intended, after he had dealt with the ancient world, to concentrate chiefly upon his own country and to come as near as he dared to modern times. In the event, the work breaks off in the third century AD. He was, he says in his Preface, uneasy about the reception of a modern history and disheartened by the death in 1612 of James's heir apparent, Prince Henry, whose interest in the project had supported and encouraged him.

The work, in its incomplete form, was published in 1614. It is carefully printed, with an engraved allegorical frontispiece and a number of maps and diagrams, and it fills nearly 800 pages in folio. It is one of the few works to which Ralegh put his name and he was promptly rebuked for his presumption. On the King's orders all copies were recalled some months after publication and not released until the title-page had been removed. Ralegh, a prisoner under sentence of death, had no business to present himself as an author. Such at least is the common interpretation of the affair, based on a theory that there was a titlepage in the first edition, as well as the engraved frontispiece, on which no author's name appears. It has recently met a lively challenge from John Racin, Jr, who cannot believe an excision would be feasible or could be effected without leaving traces in surviving copies.

Nor would the suppression of the author's name, which in any case was an open secret, have satisfied King James, who is known to have condemned the book as 'too saucy in censuring princes'. It was an article of faith with James that kings were God's vice-gerents. From this unexceptionable place he liked to move on to the respect which was therefore their due from loyal subjects. Ralegh moved in another direction. The power of kings, he delighted to point out, however great they may look in the small theatre of the world, is as nothing beside the power of God, who will exact satisfaction for all their sins. James is personally extolled as an admirable ruler, gentle of disposition and free of ancient blood-guilt, but the glib comments are lost in the grand pattern of the book, which is designed so that 'it may no less appear by evident proof than by asseveration, that ill-doing hath always been attended with ill success'.

Ralegh traces this pattern very clearly in the summary history of the kings of England which he inserts in his Preface. He found it ready made in the English chronicles, but whereas they are directed towards establishing a particular dynasty in divine favour and disestablishing rivals, Ralegh when he comes to deal with world history is more impartial. If it exasperated King James to be invited to look at himself through the wrong end of a telescope and see himself of no account, it must have been infinitely soothing to Ralegh, the prisoner in disgrace, to reduce the whole world to a scale where there was very little distinction between himself and his oppressors, except insofar as the very act of reduction, the detached clarity of vision, made him their superior. It is not for nothing that the Preface became known as *A Premonition to Princes*, and that the book ends with the famous apostrophe to Death, the Leveller:

> It is therefore Death alone that can suddenly make man to know himself. He tells the proud and insolent that they are but abjects, and humbles them at the instant; makes them cry, complain and repent, yea even to hate their forepassed happiness. He takes the accounts of the rich and proves him a beggar—a naked beggar, which has interest in nothing but the gravel that fills his mouth. He holds a glass before the eyes of the most beautiful, and makes them see therein their deformity and rottenness; and they acknowledge it. O eloquent, just and mighty Death! Whom none could advise, thou hast persuaded; what none hath dared, thou hast done; and whom all the world hath flattered, thou only

hast cast out of the world and despised. Thou hast drawn together all the far-stretched greatness, all the pride, cruelty, and ambition of man, and covered it all over with these two words *Hic Jacet*.

While Ralegh belittles man and undermines worldly values, he sets all within the structure of God's Providence. There is an order in this world, even if it is the sad one of sin and retribution. It is for this reason, and not from any idle pedantry, that he begins with the Creation and the Fall of Man. They are basic to his thesis. Thereafter he spends a long time on Bible history, since the Bible is revealed truth and makes a particularly plain demonstration of the working out of God's will. His strenuous efforts to clarify the chronology of the Old Testament and to relate it to what is otherwise known of the ancient world resulted in a series of intricate and impressive tables reproduced as an appendix to the book. From Jewish history he goes on to the Persians, the Greeks and the Romans, always following the fortunes of kings and leaders of men, the people who inaugurate policy and whose deeds have been recorded. If these, the greatest, are found wanting, it is not suggested that there will be much for which to commend their inferiors. Man is judged by his rulers. He may suffer pitiably at their hands but he shares their nature and in a position of power would not behave much differently:

Only those few black swans I must except, who having the grace to value worldly vanities at no more than their own price, do by retaining the comfortable memory of a well-acted life, behold death without dread and the grave without fear; and embrace both as necessary guides towards endless glory.

Contemporaries were delighted by the comprehensiveness of the history and did not miss, as the modern reader must, the sense of intimate participation with which Ralegh could imbue a narrative of events which fell within his own experience. This is to some extent compensated by his readiness to comment, generalize and digress. He will analyse character and motive, assess policy and dilate upon the moral implication of events, giving not only a picture of the past but of the mind of the Renaissance judging the past. He retains his power to highlight the drama of events, and if he omits the small, revealing details, it is because they have not for the most part been preserved by the earlier annalists he consulted. From time to time, though not so often as one might wish, he notes parallels in modern times and speaks of matters with which he is personally acquainted —of refugees smoked out of caves in the French wars, of the existence of Amazons in South America, of naval tactics or of the fighting qualities of the English soldier. But the main purpose of his narrative is far from that of a modern historian. It gives a view of history which is theocentric and providential, and a pessimistic assessment of man. It has therefore been dismissed by critics as conventional, 'rabbinical' and little better than medieval. This was not the opinion of contemporaries. Throughout the seventeenth century it was highly valued, because it presented a picture of life in consonance with the feeling of the times. Milton as well as Ralegh derived all history from the Creation and the Fall of Man.

In the eighteenth century it was beginning to lose ground as a historical work, though it was still valued for its piety and its excellent prose style. As a piece of writing it is the best thing Ralegh did. Ben Jonson, who was not easy to please, commended his prose, and Samuel Johnson, an equally severe critic, found it acceptable a hundred and fifty years later and distinguished it as 'elegant'. The *History* gave Ralegh considerable practice in summary narrative and terse comment. The vitality and robustness of the man are in the style, together with a detachment, due in part to his isolation from the world and from his subject matter, and in part natural to him. It is the same cool, calculating but not unsympathetic attitude that he took to the native civilizations of America, applied now to the world at large. His plainness has lost its initial awkwardness, but it derives much of its vigour from the fact that he never in his life had taken much count of formal propriety and correctness. He has no fear of sinking, and this in an age which tended to write uneasily and with excessive care.

The same absorption in direct communication ensures that when he rises it is not an empty tumescence. It is easy to select passages and label them 'purple' but it is not fair to the writer—if indeed it is fair to any good writer. At its most magnificent, Ralegh's prose still echoes his own speaking voice. It is not a falsetto. It changes because his subject has changed. His high style is at its most sustained in the Preface, its melancholy purged of excess sentiment by the note of cold disillusion. The rhythms of the long brooding sentences are extremely subtle—worthy to be set beside Donne, Browne and Milton, yet demonstrably not quite like any one of them. The mood, characteristic of its time, is a sombre stoicism, intensified rather than lightened by a vision of divine order enforced by a remote and retributive deity.

VI. 'ATHEIST'

The publication of *The History of the World*, with its pronounced if melancholy piety, removed the stigma of atheism from Ralegh's name to the satisfaction of contemporaries. Sentencing him in 1618, his judge observed; 'Your faith hath heretofore been questioned, but I am resolved you are a good Christian, for your book, which is an admirable work, doth testify as much.' One of the crowd which listened attentively to his last speech from the scaffold reported afterwards that he spoke 'not one word of Christ, but of the great and incomprehensible God, with much zeal and adoration'. The comment could be extended to *The History of the World*. Ralegh is there concerned with the source of ultimate power and ultimate order rather than with saving grace, but it is a question of emphasis not of orthodoxy.

Even a cursory glance through his writings should absolve him of the charge of atheism, which so deeply shocked his own time. It was not, however, directed against a man of letters with published work to his credit but against a royal minion, an arrogant and extravagant upstart. Ralegh had a public image upon which mud of almost any kind would stick. The Queen had given him positions of authority which he could not exercise without offence to somebody. A major cause of his unpopularity was the number of trade monopolies which had been assigned to him. He was known to be very rich. The jewels on his shoes alone were said to be worth more than £6,000. It was easy to claim that he lived in luxury at the expense of the poor and honest man. To the more obvious motives for envy and dislike, his enemies were able to add the sinister connotations of the word 'atheist'. It was used at the time as an indiscriminate term of reproach, often with no very exact theological implications. A bad man is manifestly no Christian. It could be applied as simply as that. But there were sides to Ralegh's character which on a superficial level might appear to give better justification for it. It would not otherwise have hung about him for so many years, with its murky suggestions and brimstone odour, to be exploited relentlessly in the treason trial of 1603.

The first to use it was the Jesuit, Robert Parsons, in an unflattering portrait of Elizabeth's court. His Latin pamphlet was widely read. A summary in English, published in 1592, speaks of 'Sir Walter Ralegh's school of atheism and the conjuror who is master thereof and of the great diligence used to draw young gentlemen to this school'. The writer seems to have been reflecting on Ralegh's interest in the physical sciences, in particular mathematics, as taught by a notable scholar, Thomas Harriot. Mathematical studies followed naturally from his practical concern with navigation and cartography. Harriot, whom he maintained as a member of his household, can be plausibly identified as his 'conjuror'. He was one of the most advanced astronomers of his day and carried to his grave the odium which tended to accompany a man who probed God's mysteries in the physical universe.

As well as being a patron of Harriot, Ralegh was said to have been one of those to whom Marlowe 'read the atheist lecture', and upon this slender foundation there has been built a supposition that he and Marlowe were closely acquainted. A theory with more substance is that both men were involved in a libertine circle known as the School of Night. This has recently become a critical commonplace. It is worth examining the foundation upon which it is built. Father Parsons, in a hostile pamphlet, spoke of Ralegh's 'school of atheism'. So much is fact. From there the commentators go on to equate 'school of atheism' with the phrase 'school of night', which is used by Shakespeare in *Love's Labour's Lost*, buried deep among some rather obvious pleasantries upon the hackneyed theme of fair and dark beauty. Biron is mocked because he has fallen in love with a Dark Lady. 'Fie', cries the King of Navarre,

> black is the badge of Hell,
> The hue of dungeons, and the School of night.

This solitary, unemphatic, rather mysterious phrase has been used, with the help of much ingenious argument, to prove the play a satire upon Ralegh and his associates and their scientific studies. The argument, in fact, can stand without reference to 'the school of night', though it is harder without it to bring in Ralegh. Shakespeare mocks pedants, who as plodders and killjoys have never found favour in comedy, and suggests that young men find their stars in women's eyes. The question may then be propounded whether he had any particular person or persons in mind, who they were and what kind of audience would understand and enjoy sallies at their expense.

In 1594, rumours of atheism followed Ralegh to Dorset where he had retired to his country house at Sherborne. An ecclesiastical commission was sent to investigate, perhaps to protect rather than to convict him. Anyhow, no prosecution followed, nor did the evidence warrant it. The heart of his offending seems to have been that at a dinner party he and his brother Sir Carew baited a conventional parson, the Revd. William Ironside. Ralegh took up the position, theologically unexceptionable, that man cannot define the substance of the soul. The parson, unwilling to be put down by a layman, retorted with logic, and Ralegh proceeded to tie him in knots. Ernest Strathmann thinks that in essence the dispute was concerned with the validity of Aristotelian logic and hardly with theology at all, and that Ironside knew the local gossips had misinterpreted it. The consequences show that Ralegh was playing a dangerous game and it is not likely to have been the first time he had played it. He enjoyed argument and had a gift for it. He would have done well to walk more circumspectly, but circumspection was never a characteristic of his. Infinitely plausible and warmly sympathetic when he was so disposed, he could on occasion be tactless and wantonly indiscreet. He had the intelligent man's confidence that truth speaks for itself and he was contemptuous of commonplace minds.

Ralegh was interested in the problems propounded by the nature of God, of creation and of the image of God in man. They bulk largely in *The History of the World*, especially in the second chapter. *A Treatise of the Soul*, said to be his work, was printed from a manuscript copy in 1820. A minor piece called *Sceptick* was one of the first of his papers to be published and appeared regularly with his *Remains*. It is a collection of notes from Sextus Empiricus, and is confined to showing the imperfections of human knowledge. A philosophical position such as this can very easily be accompanied by faith in an inscrutable deity. Indeed it was regularly used by polemicists to throw man back upon God, all human props having been proved fallible. It is peculiarly liable to be misconstrued by narrow minds. Ralegh had a dangerous kind of disengagement, a tolerance when confronted with alien ideas and an intellectual boldness. It is not hard to imagine him listening to Marlowe reading 'the atheist lecture'.

Over and above this, his own beliefs are marked by an austerity unlikely to recommend them to simpler minds and warmer hearts. He is constant, for instance, in his assertion that immortal souls are completely severed from all human concerns:

> But hereof we are assured, that the long and dark night of death ... shall cover us over till the world be no more. After which, and when we shall again receive organs glorified and incorruptible, the seats of angelical affections: in so great admiration shall the souls of the blessed be exercised as they cannot admit the mixture of any second or less joy, nor any return of foregone or mortal affection, towards friends, kindred, children. Of whom whether we shall retain any particular knowledge, or in any sort distinguish them, no man can assure us: and the wisest men doubt.

In his farewell letter to his wife, when he awaited the death-stroke in 1603, this became 'As for me, I am no more yours, nor you mine. Death hath cut us assunder: and God hath divided me from the world, and you from me'. Gentle and practical, he begs her not to have scruples about marrying again, 'For that will be best for you: both in respect of God and the world'.

It is not always realized how profoundly unsentimental Ralegh was, even to hardness. This comes out very clearly in his brief *Instructions to his Son*, which almost all readers find too apt to recommend self-interest. In politics he had a kind of machiavellian realism, in which he differs from his fellow Elizabethans only in being more articulate. Many of his actions seem to contradict it. He was not a very shrewd politician and allowed himself to be outmanœuvred. He stood by the old Queen, for instance, when self-interest should have sent him where the rest were going, to her probable heir. They quietly and industriously undermined him. In popular belief machiavellian craft was as characteristic of him as atheism. He was the arch-plotter. Melodrama lit him luridly. At his trial he was addressed as 'monster', 'viper' and 'spider of hell'. Yet he had done much to advance his country and help his countrymen, notably the seamen and the west-country tinners. He was concerned with tin mining as Lord Warden of the Stannaries. As Vice-Admiral of Devon and Cornwall he had charge of the Admiralty Courts. He had served his time as a member of parliament, where he spoke up for the underprivileged, against witch-hunts among nonconformists and against taxing the poor. It was a matter of regret to him that he was never a member of the Privy Council.

During his imprisonment he wrote some able treatises upon current affairs. *The Prerogative of Parliaments* is an imaginary discussion in which a Justice of the Peace shows a rather haughty Councillor that an English king must rule through his parliament or disregard it at his peril. As advice to a reigning Stuart, trying his best to bypass his parliaments, it was more timely than tactful. It appeared in 1628 under a foreign imprint. Prince Henry asked him to summarize the arguments against the pro-Spanish marriages which were proposed for the prince and his sister. These pamphlets are vigorous, orderly and spare, not without the flash of anecdote or phrase with which Ralegh almost always lights up his arguments. It is he, for instance, who tells how Essex fatally alienated the Queen by blurting out in a temper that 'her conditions were as crooked as her carcase'. Elsewhere he regrets that she had not 'believed her men of war, as she did her scribes' for then they would have made the kings of Spain 'Kings of Figs and oranges, as in old times'. A very Raleghan discourse, on a wider and more general subject, is *The Miseries of War*. It is typical of the disillusioned historian seeing through the pretences of mankind. The Ralegh who none the less urged the exploitation of Guiana and pressed the war with Spain was, on his own admission, no more than human. 'Of a long time my course was a course of vanity', he said in his last speech from the scaffold. 'I have been a seafaring man, a soldier, and a courtier, and in the temptations of the least of these there is enough to overthrow a good mind, and a good man.'

His character is far from simple, and though much information is available about his life it is often too fragmentary to solve the contradictions, which may lie at deep levels. In his writing he combines cynicism with idealism, truth with fiction, and a sombre pessimism with a contagious zest for life.

SIR WALTER RALEGH

A Select Bibliography

(Place of publication London, unless stated otherwise)

Bibliography:
THE BIBLIOGRAPHY OF SIR WALTER RALEGH, by T. N. Brushfield; Exeter (1886)
—reprinted from *The Western Antiquary*; second ed. 1908.

Collected Works:
JUDICIOUS AND SELECT ESSAYES AND OBSERVATIONS UPON THE FIRST INVENTION OF SHIPPING, THE MISERY OF INVASIVE WARRE, THE NAVY ROYALL AND SEA-SERVICE [authorship queried, see H. E. Sandison, *Arthur Gorges*, 1928]; WITH HIS APOLOGIE FOR HIS VOYAGE TO GUIANA (1650).
SCEPTICK, OR SPECULATIONS; AND OBSERVATIONS OF THE MAGNIFICENCY AND OPULENCY OF CITIES; HIS SEAT OF GOVERNMENT; AND LETTERS TO THE KING'S MAJESTIE, AND OTHERS OF QUALITIE [and also three poems: i. 'The Passionate Man's Pilgrimage'; ii. 'Even Such is Time'; iii. 'On the Snuff of a Candle']; ALSO HIS DEMEANOR BEFORE HIS EXECUTION [i.e. his last speech]. (1651)
—subsequently reprinted as *Remains* (see next entry). On the authorship of *Sceptick*, see S. E. Sprott, *Philological Quarterly*, April 1963.
REMAINS OF SIR WALTER RALEIGH (1651-1702)
—the editions between 1651 and 1702 contain in various combinations the items in the 1651 volume together with *His Instructions to his Sonne; and The Son's Advice to his aged father* [first published 1632, the second item almost certainly spurious]; *Maxims of State* [first published 1642]; *Observations touching Trade and Commerce with the Hollander* [first published 1653. Authorship queried, see A. Buff, *Englische Studien*, 1877]; *The Prerogative of Parliaments in England* [first published Middelburg and Hamburg 1628].
THREE DISCOURSES: I. OF A WAR WITH SPAIN, AND OUR PROTECTING THE NETHERLANDS; II. OF THE ORIGINAL AND FUNDAMENTAL CAUSE OF NATURAL, ARBITRARY AND CIVIL WAR; III. OF ECCLESIASTICAL POWER (1702)
—the last two discourses appeared in 1650 as *The Misery of Invasive Warre*. The section in Discourse II on *Civil or Unnatural War* is new.

THE WORKS: Political, Commercial and Philosophical, together with his letters and poems . . . to which is prefix'd a new account of his life, by T. Birch, 2 vols (1751)
—does not include the *History of the World*, but adds to works previously collected some new poems and letters and *The Cabinet Council containing the Chief Arts of Empire and Mysteries of State* (1658), published as *Aphorisms of State* (1661) and as *The Arts of Empire and the Secrets of Government* (1697). [Authorship queried by E. Strathmann, *Times Literary Supplement*, 13 April 1956]; *A Discourse touching a Match propounded by the Savoyan, between the Lady Elizabeth and the Prince of Piedmont; A Discourse touching a Marriage between Prince Henry of England, and a Daughter of Savoy* [first published as *The Interest of England with regard to Foreign Alliances*, 1750]; *A Voyage for the Discovery of Guiana; An Introduction to a Breviary of the History of England with the Reign of King William the I* [first published 1693, authorship queried, see R. B. Gottfried, *Studies in Philology*, April 1956].

THE WORKS OF SIR WALTER RALEGH, KT NOW FIRST COLLECTED: to which are prefixed the lives of the author, by William Oldys and Thomas Birch. 8 vols; Oxford (1829)
—Vol. I. *Lives*. Vol. II–VII. *The History of the World*. Vol. VIII contains all the minor works in the edition of 1751 with some smaller pieces, including *A Relation of Cadiz Action* [first printed with the abridged *History of the World*, 1700]; *A Treatise of the Soul*. The collection of poems is supplemented from Sir E. Brydges's unreliable Lee Priory Press edition (see below). Reprinted New York 1965.

Selected Works:

THE POEMS, ed. Sir E. Brydges (1813)
—privately printed at the editor's Lee Priory Press, Kent.

POEMS BY SIR HENRY WOTTON, SIR WALTER RALEIGH, AND OTHERS, ed. J. Hannah (1845)
—Pickering's attractively printed anthology.

THE COURTLY POETS FROM RALEIGH TO MONTROSE, ed. J. Hannah (1870)
—published in the Aldine edition of the British Poets.

SELECTIONS, ed. G. E. Hadow; Oxford (1917)
—contains excerpts from *The History of the World*, the whole of *The Last Fight of the Revenge, Cadiz Action*, and some letters.

POEMS, ed. A. M. C. Latham (1929)
—revised and supplemented, 1951. The standard text.
SILVER POETS OF THE SIXTEENTH CENTURY, ed. G. Bullett (1947).
SELECTED PROSE AND POETRY, ed. A. M. C. Latham (1965).

Separate Works:
A REPORT OF THE TRUTH OF THE FIGHT ABOUT THE ILES OF AÇORES, THIS LAST SUMMER. BETWIXT THE REVENGE ONE OF HER MAJESTIES SHIPPES AND AN ARMADA OF THE KING OF SPAINE (1591)
—reprinted in Hakluyt's *Voyages*, Vol. II (1599), and in Arber's *English Reprints* (1908). Not included by Birch or in the Oxford *Works*.

THE DISCOVERIE OF THE LARGE, RICH, AND BEWTIFUL EMPIRE OF GUIANA (3 eds, 1596)
—reprinted in Hakluyt's *Voyages*, Vol. III (1598). Edited by R. H. Schomburgk with valuable topographical notes, a transcript of Ralegh's autograph journal of the voyage, and 'Considerations on the Voyage to Guiana' said to be by Ralegh but more probably by Lawrence Keymis (1848). Edited by V. T. Harlow, 1928, with an excellent introduction, transcripts from Spanish documents, and a reproduction of one of Ralegh's maps, BM Add. MS 17940 A.

THE HISTORY OF THE WORLD. IN FIVE BOOKES (1614)
—9 editions before 1700. Reprinted by W. Oldys, 2 vols, 1736. Abridged as *The Marrow of Historie* (1650) and as *An Abridgment of Sir Walter Raleigh's History* (1698).

Some Biographical and Critical Studies:
FRAGMENTA REGALIA, by Sir R. Naunton (1641)
—ed. E. Arber, 1895.

THE ARRAIGNMENT AND CONVICTION OF SIR WALTER RAWLEIGH, copied by Sir T. Overbury (1648).

THE LIFE OF SIR WALTER RALEGH, by W. Oldys (1736)
—prefixed to *The History of the World*, reprinted in *Works*, 1829.

THE LIFE OF SIR WALTER RALEGH, by T. Birch (1751)
—prefixed to *Collected Works*, reprinted in *Works*, 1829.

THE LIFE OF SIR WALTER RALEGH, by A. Cayley, 2 vols (1805).

COBBETT'S COMPLETE COLLECTION OF STATE TRIALS, Vol. II (1809).

'The Case against Sir Walter Ralegh', by S. R. Gardiner, *The Fortnightly Review*, n.s.I., 1867.

THE LIFE OF SIR W. RALEGH . . . TOGETHER WITH HIS LETTERS, by E. Edwards, 2 vols (1868)
—a standard work, well documented, providing the only substantial collection of Ralegh's letters.

SIR WALTER RALEGH: A Biography, by W. Stebbing; Oxford (1891)
—one of the best of the biographies of Ralegh; second ed., 1899.

DRAKE AND THE TUDOR NAVY, by J. S. Corbett, 2 vols (1898).

THE SUCCESSORS OF DRAKE, by J. S. Corbett (1900).

THE NAVAL TRACTS OF SIR W. MONSON, ed. M. Oppenheim, 5 vols (1902)
—Publications of the Navy Record Society, Vols XXII, XXIII, XLIII, XLV, XLIX.

'Sir Walter Ralegh's *History of the World*', by C. H. Firth, *Proceedings of the British Academy*, 1917-18
—reprinted in *Essays Historical and Literary*, Oxford, 1938.

'The Battle of Flores', by G. Callender, *History*, 1919.

WILLOBIE HIS AVISA, by H. Willoby with an essay by G. B. Harrison (1926)
—prints in full the evidence before the commission enquiring into atheism in Dorset.

RALEGHS STAATSTHEORETISCHE SCHRIFTEN: DIE EINFÜHRUNG DES MACHIAVELLISMUS IN ENGLAND, by N. Kempner; Leipzig (1928).

'Un machiavellico Inglese: Sir Walter Raleigh', by M. Praz, *La Cultura*, January 1929.

RALEGH'S LAST VOYAGE, by V. T. Harlow (1932)
—reprints almost all available documents except Ralegh's journal.

ATHEISM IN THE ENGLISH RENAISSANCE, by G. T. Buckley; Chicago (1932).

'La Religion de Sir Walter Ralegh', by J. Beau, *Revue Anglo-Américaine*, June 1934.

LATE TUDOR AND EARLY STUART GEOGRAPHY, 1583-1650, by E. G. R. Taylor (1934).

SIR WALTER RALEGH: the last of the Elizabethans, by E. Thompson (1935).

THE SCHOOL OF NIGHT: A Study in the literary relationships of Sir Walter Ralegh, by M. C. Bradbrook; Cambridge (1936).

'Sir Walter Ralegh as Poet and Philosopher', by C. F. Tucker Brooke, *English Literary History*, June 1938
—reprinted in *Essays on Shakespeare*, 1948.

'The Sixteenth-Century Lyric in England', by Y. Winters, *Poetry* (Chicago), 1938-9.

'The Textual Evidence for "The School of Night"', by E. A. Strathmann, *Modern Language Notes*, Vol. LVI, No. 3, March 1941.

RALEIGH AND THE BRITISH EMPIRE, by D. B. Quinn (1947)
—for Ralegh's Virginian Colony, see the same author's *The Roanoke Voyages, 1584-1590*, 2 vols, 1955.

'Sir Walter Ralegh's Goldmine', by A. M. C. Latham, *Essays and Studies*, 1951.

SIR WALTER RALEGH: A Study in Elizabethan Skepticism, by E. A. Strathmann; New York (1951)
—an admirably detailed and documented study.

'The Working Papers for The History of the World', by W. F. Oakeshott, *The Times*, 29 November 1952.

SIR WALTER RALEIGH, by P. Edwards (1953)
—a general study of Ralegh as a literary figure.

THE OXFORD HISTORY OF ENGLISH LITERATURE; Oxford (1945-)
—Vol. III, *English Literature in the 16th Century*, by C. S. Lewis, 1954. Bk III, iii, contains comment on Ralegh.

THE PELICAN GUIDE TO ENGLISH LITERATURE, ed. B. Ford (1955)
—Vol II, *The Age of Shakespeare*, contains a chapter 'Two Elizabethan Poets: Daniel and Ralegh', by P. Ure.

ELIZABETHAN POETRY, ed. J. R. Brown and B. Harris (1960)
—Stratford-upon-Avon Studies, No. 2. Contains an essay 'A Reading of the Ocean's Love to Cynthia', by D. Davie. The original MS of this fragmentary poem survives at Hatfield House.

THE QUEEN AND THE POET, by W. F. Oakeshott (1960)
—a detailed study of Ralegh's poetry against the background of his life.

ENGLISH LITERATURE IN THE EARLIER SEVENTEENTH CENTURY, by D. Bush; Oxford (1945)
—second ed., 1962.

RALEGH AND THE THROCKMORTONS, by A. L. Rowse (1962)
—contains decisive evidence of Ralegh's marriage. See also F. Sorensen, 'Sir Walter Ralegh's Marriage', *Studies in Philology*, Vol. XXXIII, No. 2, April 1936, and P. Lefranc, 'La date du mariage de Sir Walter Ralegh', *Études Anglaises*, July-Sept. 1956.

'The Early Editions of Sir Walter Ralegh's *The History of the World*' by John Racin, Jr. *Studies in Bibliography*, 1964.

SIR WALTER RALEIGH, by N. L. Williams (1965).
—with copious quotations from contemporary documents.

INTELLECTUAL ORIGINS OF THE ENGLISH REVOLUTION, by J. E. C. Hill (1965)
—the influence of Ralegh's writings upon the later seventeenth century.

SIR WALTER RALEIGH ÉCRIVAIN: l'œuvre et les idées, by P. Lefranc; Paris (1968)
—the most thorough treatment yet accorded to Ralegh as writer and thinker.

THE SHEPHERD OF THE OCEAN: An Account of Sir Walter Raleigh and his times, by J. H. Adamson and H. F. Folland (1969)

WRITERS AND THEIR WORK

General Surveys:
THE DETECTIVE STORY IN BRITAIN: Julian Symons
THE ENGLISH BIBLE: Donald Coggan
ENGLISH VERSE EPIGRAM: G. Rostrevor Hamilton
ENGLISH HYMNS: A. Pollard
ENGLISH MARITIME WRITING: Hakluyt to Cook: Oliver Warner
THE ENGLISH SHORT STORY I: & II: T. O. Beachcroft
THE ENGLISH SONNET: P. Cruttwell
ENGLISH SERMONS: Arthur Pollard
ENGLISH TRANSLATORS and TRANSLATIONS: J. M. Cohen
ENGLISH TRAVELLERS IN THE NEAR EAST: Robin Fedden
THREE WOMEN DIARISTS: M. Willy

Sixteenth Century and Earlier:
FRANCIS BACON: J. Max Patrick
BEAUMONT & FLETCHER: Ian Fletcher
CHAUCER: Nevill Coghill
GOWER & LYDGATE: Derek Pearsall
RICHARD HOOKER: A. Pollard
THOMAS KYD: Philip Edwards
LANGLAND: Nevill Coghill
LYLY & PEELE: G. K. Hunter
MALORY: M. C. Bradbrook
MARLOWE: Philip Henderson
SIR THOMAS MORE: E. E. Reynolds
RALEGH: Agnes Latham
SIDNEY: Kenneth Muir
SKELTON: Peter Green
SPENSER: Rosemary Freeman
THREE 14TH-CENTURY ENGLISH MYSTICS: Phyllis Hodgson
TWO SCOTS CHAUCERIANS: H. Harvey Wood
WYATT: Sergio Baldi

Seventeenth Century:
SIR THOMAS BROWNE: Peter Green
BUNYAN: Henri Talon
CAVALIER POETS: Robin Skelton
CONGREVE: Bonamy Dobrée
DONNE: F. Kermode
DRYDEN: Bonamy Dobrée
ENGLISH DIARISTS: Evelyn and Pepys: M. Willy
FARQUHAR: A. J. Farmer
JOHN FORD: Clifford Leech
GEORGE HERBERT: T. S. Eliot
HERRICK: John Press
HOBBES: T. E. Jessop
BEN JONSON: J. B. Bamborough
LOCKE: Maurice Cranston
ANDREW MARVELL: John Press
MILTON: E. M. W. Tillyard
RESTORATION COURT POETS: V. de S. Pinto
SHAKESPEARE: C. J. Sisson
  CHRONICLES: Clifford Leech
  EARLY COMEDIES: Derek Traversi
  LATER COMEDIES: G. K. Hunter
  FINAL PLAYS: F. Kermode
  HISTORIES: L. C. Knights
  POEMS: F. T. Prince
  PROBLEM PLAYS: Peter Ure
  ROMAN PLAYS: T. J. B. Spencer
  GREAT TRAGEDIES: Kenneth Muir
THREE METAPHYSICAL POETS: Margaret Willy
WEBSTER: Ian Scott-Kilvert
WYCHERLEY: P. F. Vernon

Eighteenth Century:
BERKELEY: T. E. Jessop
BLAKE: Kathleen Raine
BOSWELL: P. A. W. Collins
BURKE: T. E. Utley
BURNS: David Daiches
WM. COLLINS: Oswald Doughty
COWPER: N. Nicholson
CRABBE: R. L. Brett
DEFOE: J. R. Sutherland
FIELDING: John Butt
GAY: Oliver Warner
GIBBON: C. V. Wedgwood
GOLDSMITH: A. Norman Jeffares
GRAY: R. W. Ketton-Cremer
HUME: Montgomery Belgion
SAMUEL JOHNSON: S. C. Roberts
POPE: Ian Jack
RICHARDSON: R. F. Brissenden
SHERIDAN: W. A. Darlington
CHRISTOPHER SMART: G. Grigson
SMOLLETT: Laurence Brander
STEELE, ADDISON: A. R. Humphreys
STERNE: D. W. Jefferson
SWIFT: J. Middleton Murry
SIR JOHN VANBRUGH: Bernard Harris
HORACE WALPOLE: Hugh Honour

Nineteenth Century:
MATTHEW ARNOLD: Kenneth Allott
JANE AUSTEN: S. Townsend Warner
BAGEHOT: N. St John-Stevas
BRONTË SISTERS: Phyllis Bentley
BROWNING: John Bryson
E. B. BROWNING: Alethea Hayter
SAMUEL BUTLER: G. D. H. Cole

BYRON: Bernard Blackstone
CARLYLE: David Gascoyne
LEWIS CARROLL: Derek Hudson
COLERIDGE: Kathleen Raine
CREEVEY & GREVILLE: J. Richardson
DE QUINCEY: Hugh Sykes Davies
DICKENS: K. J. Fielding
  EARLY NOVELS: T. Blount
  LATER NOVELS: B. Hardy
DISRAELI: Paul Bloomfield
GEORGE ELIOT: Lettice Cooper
FERRIER & GALT: W. M. Parker
FITZGERALD: Joanna Richardson
ELIZABETH GASKELL: Miriam Allott
GISSING: A. C. Ward
THOMAS HARDY: R. A. Scott-James
    and C. Day Lewis
HAZLITT: J. B. Priestley
HOOD: Laurence Brander
G. M. HOPKINS: Geoffrey Grigson
T. H. HUXLEY: William Irvine
KEATS: Edmund Blunden
LAMB: Edmund Blunden
LANDOR: G. Rostrevor Hamilton
EDWARD LEAR: Joanna Richardson
MACAULAY: G. R. Potter
MEREDITH: Phyllis Bartlett
JOHN STUART MILL: M. Cranston
WILLIAM MORRIS: P. Henderson
NEWMAN: J. M. Cameron
PATER: Ian Fletcher
PEACOCK: J. I. M. Stewart
ROSSETTI: Oswald Doughty
CHRISTINA ROSSETTI: G. Battiscombe
RUSKIN: Peter Quennell
SIR WALTER SCOTT: Ian Jack
SHELLEY: G. M. Matthews
SOUTHEY: Geoffrey Carnall
LESLIE STEPHEN: Phyllis Grosskurth
R. L. STEVENSON: G. B. Stern
SWINBURNE: H. J. C. Grierson
TENNYSON: B. C. Southam
THACKERAY: Laurence Brander
FRANCIS THOMPSON: P. Butter
TROLLOPE: Hugh Sykes Davies
OSCAR WILDE: James Laver
WORDSWORTH: Helen Darbishire

Twentieth Century:
CHINUA ACHEBE: A. Ravenscroft
W. H. AUDEN: Richard Hoggart
HILAIRE BELLOC: Renée Haynes
ARNOLD BENNETT: F. Swinnerton
EDMUND BLUNDEN: Alec M. Hardie
ROBERT BRIDGES: J. Sparrow
ROY CAMPBELL: David Wright
JOYCE CARY: Walter Allen
G. K. CHESTERTON: C. Hollis

WINSTON CHURCHILL: John Connell
R. G. COLLINGWOOD: E. W. F. Tomlin
I. COMPTON-BURNETT:
    R. Glynn Grylls
JOSEPH CONRAD: Oliver Warner
WALTER DE LA MARE: K. Hopkins
NORMAN DOUGLAS: Ian Greenlees
LAWRENCE DURRELL: G. S. Fraser
T. S. ELIOT: M. C. Bradbrook
FIRBANK & BETJEMAN: J. Brooke
FORD MADOX FORD: Kenneth Young
E. M. FORSTER: Rex Warner
CHRISTOPHER FRY: Derek Stanford
JOHN GALSWORTHY: R. H. Mottram
WM. GOLDING: Clive Pemberton
ROBERT GRAVES: M. Seymour-Smith
GRAHAM GREENE: Francis Wyndham
L. P. HARTLEY: Paul Bloomfield
A. E. HOUSMAN: Ian Scott-Kilvert
ALDOUS HUXLEY: Jocelyn Brooke
HENRY JAMES: Michael Swan
PAMELA HANSFORD JOHNSON:
    Isabel Quigly
JAMES JOYCE: J. I. M. Stewart
RUDYARD KIPLING: Bonamy Dobrée
D. H. LAWRENCE: Kenneth Young
C. DAY LEWIS: Clifford Dyment
WYNDHAM LEWIS: E. W. F. Tomlin
COMPTON MACKENZIE: K. Young
LOUIS MACNEICE: John Press
KATHERINE MANSFIELD: Ian Gordon
JOHN MASEFIELD: L. A. G. Strong
SOMERSET MAUGHAM: J. Brophy
GEORGE MOORE: A. Norman Jeffares
J. MIDDLETON MURRY: Philip Mairet
SEAN O'CASEY: W. A. Armstrong
GEORGE ORWELL: Tom Hopkinson
JOHN OSBORNE: Simon Trussler
HAROLD PINTER: John Russell Taylor
POETS OF 1939-45 WAR: R. N. Currey
POWYS BROTHERS: R. C. Churchill
J. B. PRIESTLEY: Ivor Brown
HERBERT READ: Francis Berry
FOUR REALIST NOVELISTS: V. Brome
BERNARD SHAW: A. C. Ward
EDITH SITWELL: John Lehmann
KENNETH SLESSOR: C. Semmler
C. P. SNOW: William Cooper
SYNGE & LADY GREGORY: E. Coxhead
DYLAN THOMAS: G. S. Fraser
G. M. TREVELYAN: J. H. Plumb
WAR POETS: 1914-18: E. Blunden
EVELYN WAUGH: Christopher Hollis
H. G. WELLS: Montgomery Belgion
PATRICK WHITE: R. F. Brissenden
ANGUS WILSON: K. W. Gransden
VIRGINIA WOOLF: B. Blackstone
W. B. YEATS: G. S. Fraser